Dan Cederholm

SASS FOR WEB DESIGNERS

Publisher: Jeffrey Zeldman
Designer: Jason Santa Maria
Editor-in-Chief: Mandy Brown
Editor: Erin Kissane
Technical Editor: Jina Bolton
Copyeditor: Tina Lee
Compositor: Rob Weychert
Ebook Production: India Amos

ISBN: 978-1-9375571-2-6

A Book Apart
New York, New York
http://abookapart.com

10 9 8 7 6 5 4 3 2 1

TABLE OF CONTENTS

FOREWORD

LOOKING BACK at the evolution of computer languages, it seems every dozen years or so a new layer of abstraction is added. "Ones and zeros" leveled up into assembly instructions, which leveled up into compiled languages. Those compiled languages evolved and we used them to create web browsers. Web browsers digest languages like HTML, CSS, and JavaScript. Now we're ready to level up again.

HTML, CSS, and JavaScript have been *enormously* successful languages for moving the web forward in unprecedented ways. We're building ever-bigger and more complex websites. That's a beautiful thing. But we've come to the point where we need to take the next step in making what we build more manageable and maintainable. We can get there through abstraction.

CSS is in the most dire need. These days, HTML is generally produced through backend code and templates which provide the abstraction we need. As a programming language, JavaScript already has the tools of abstraction baked in. CSS has no abstraction at all and is highly repetitive. While that simplicity was key to its adoption, it makes it unwieldy for us today. It's CSS's turn to level up!

Sass, as Dan will teach you in this book, has all the tools of abstraction we need. Repetitive values become variables. Repetitive groups of styles become extends. Complex rulesets and tedious vendor prefixing become mixins. With those translations comes CSS that is manageable and maintainable at any scale.

Moving to Sass isn't a comfortable transition for some. Dan knows that all too well. He has been working with and teaching CSS to the world since before I knew what a `div` was. But Dan is a craftsman of the web. Just as a craftsman of wood knows when his chisel is dull, Dan knew that working directly in CSS these days is just like that dull chisel: you can do it, but you're liable to hurt yourself.

By the time you finish this book and give Sass a real try on your first project, you'll be a master of 95% of the important, truly value-adding parts of Sass. Let Dan be your guide. Learn that Sass doesn't make your job harder, it makes it easier.

—Chris Coyier

1

WHY SASS?

I WAS A reluctant believer in Sass. I write stylesheets by hand! I don't need help! And I certainly don't want to add extra complexity to my workflow. Go away!

That was the thinking anyway. But the reality is that Sass (and other CSS preprocessors) can be a powerful ally—a tool that any style-crafter can easily insert into their daily work. It took me a while to come around, but I'm sure glad that I did.

And that's the reason I wanted to write this little book. To share how I've been able to use Sass to be more efficient, while maintaining the process I've become comfortable with from writing CSS for the last ten years. I had many misconceptions about Sass that prevented me from giving it a go, initially. I was worried I'd have to completely alter the way I write and manage stylesheets. As CSS can be fragile at times, it's understandable for its authors to be somewhat protective about their creation. Can I get an amen?

Ahem.

So, I'm here to show you how Sass doesn't have to disrupt your process and workflow, and how it can make your life easier. I'll demonstrate the various aspects of Sass, how to install it, how to use it, and how it's helped me in my own projects. With any luck, I just might make you a believer as well.

THE SASS ELEVATOR PITCH

Ever needed to change, say, a color in your stylesheet, and found that you had to find and replace the value multiple times? Don't you wish CSS allowed you to do this?

```
$brand-color: #fc3;

a {
  color: $brand-color;
}
nav {
  background-color: $brand-color;
}
```

What if you could change that value in one place and the entire stylesheet reflected that change? You can with Sass!

Or how about repeated blocks of styles that are used in various locations throughout the stylesheet?

```
p {
  margin-bottom: 20px;
  font-size: 14px;
  line-height: 1.5;
}
footer {
  margin-bottom: 20px;
  font-size: 14px;
  line-height: 1.5;
}
```

Wouldn't it be fantastic to roll those shared rules into a reusable block? Again, defined only once but included wherever you needed them.

```
@mixin default-type {
  margin-bottom: 20px;
  font-size: 14px;
  line-height: 1.5;
}

p {
  @include default-type;
}
footer {
  @include default-type;
}
```

That's also Sass! And those two extremely simple examples barely scratch the surface as to how Sass makes authoring stylesheets faster, easier, and more flexible. It's a welcome helper in the world of web design, because anyone that's created a website knows...

CSS IS HARD

Let's face it: learning CSS isn't easy. Understanding what each property does, how the cascade works, which browser supports what, the selectors, the quirks, and so forth. It's not easy. Add on top of that the complexity of the interfaces we're building these days, and the maintenance that goes along with that and—wait, why are we doing this again? It's a puzzle, and some of us enjoy the eventual completion.

Part of the problem is that CSS wasn't originally designed to do the things we do with it today. Sure, progress is moving along at a nice clip thanks to rapid browser innovation and implementation of CSS3 and beyond. But we still need to rely on techniques that are, for all intents and purposes, hacks. The float property, for example, was designed to simply align an image within a block of text. That's it. Yet we've had to bend that property to lay out entire interfaces.

Our stylesheets are also immensely repetitive. Colors, fonts, oft-used groupings of properties, etc. The typical CSS file is an extremely linear document—the kind of thing that makes an object-oriented programmer want to tear their hair out. (I'm not an object-oriented programmer, but I have very little hair left. Read into that as you may).

As interfaces and web applications become more robust and complex, we're bending the original design of CSS to do things it never dreamed of doing. We're crafty like that. Fortunately, browser makers adopt new CSS features far more rapidly these days, with more efficient and powerful properties and selectors that solve the problems today's web poses. Features like new layout options in CSS3, `border-radius`, `box-shadow`, advanced selectors, transitions, transforms, animation, and so on. It's an exciting time. And yet, there's still a lot missing from CSS itself. There are holes to be plugged, and the life of a stylesheet author should be a lot easier.

The DRY principle

If we peer into the world of software engineering (and I much prefer to peer than hang out and get comfortable there), we can quickly see how organization, variables, constants, partials, etc., are an ingrained, crucial way of working for folks building complex systems.

You may have heard of the "don't repeat yourself" (DRY) principle. Coined and defined by Andy Hunt and Dave Thomas in their book, *The Pragmatic Programmer* (http://bkaprt.com/sass/1/), DRY declares:

> *Every piece of knowledge must have a single, unambiguous, authoritative representation within a system.*

The idea is that duplicating code can cause failure and confusion for developers (http://bkaprt.com/sass/2/). It's common sense as well: write commonly-repeated patterns once, and reuse those bits throughout the application. It's more efficient and far easier to maintain code this way.

CSS is anything but DRY. At times, it drips with repeated rules, declarations, and values. We're constantly writing the same snippets of code for colors, fonts, and frequently-used patterns of style throughout our stylesheets. One look through a decent-sized CSS file, and a DRY software developer will weep, first with bewilderment, then frustration.

"How the !@#$ do you maintain this?!" they'll ask.

"Have I also told you about IE bugs?" you'll reply with a bit of self-loathing.

So why is CSS so difficult to work with?

We can gather a hint of understanding why CSS has had its syntax limitations over the years from an essay by CSS co-inventor, Bert Bos (http://bkaprt.com/sass/3/):

> CSS stops short of even more powerful features that programmers use in their programming languages: macros, variables, symbolic constants, conditionals, expressions over variables, etc. That is because these things give power-users a lot of rope, but less experienced users will unwittingly hang themselves; or, more likely, be so scared that they won't even touch CSS. It's a balance. And for CSS the balance is different than for some other things.

The original architects of CSS were concerned with adoption. They (rightfully) wanted as many people as possible creating websites. They wanted CSS to be powerful enough to style web pages and separate content from presentation, while being easy to understand and use. I can certainly respect that. At the same time, we have work to do, and that work is getting more complicated, more nuanced, and more challenging to maintain and to future-proof.

Fortunately, there are options to help us out here, and one of them is Sass.

WHAT IS SASS?

Sass is a CSS preprocessor—a layer between the stylesheets you author and the `.css` files you serve to the browser. Sass (short for Syntactically Awesome Stylesheets) plugs the holes in CSS as a language, allowing you to write DRY code that'll be faster, more efficient, and easier to maintain (**FIG 1**).

The Sass website (http://bkaprt.com/sass/4/) describes itself succinctly:

> Sass is a meta-language on top of CSS that's used to describe the style of a document cleanly and structurally, with more power than flat CSS allows. Sass both provides a simpler, more elegant syntax for CSS and implements various features that are useful for creating manageable stylesheets.

So while normal CSS doesn't yet allow things like variables, mixins (reusable blocks of styles), and other goodies, Sass provides a syntax that does all of that and more—enabling "super functionality" in addition to your normal CSS. It then translates (or compiles) that syntax into regular ol' CSS files via a command-line program or web-framework plugin.

More specifically, Sass is an extension of CSS3, and its SCSS ("Sassy CSS") syntax—which we'll talk about in just a moment—is a superset of CSS3. Meaning, any valid CSS3 document is a valid SCSS document as well. This is integral to Sass being something you can "ease into." Getting started with Sass syntax is painless, and you can use as little or as much as you'd like. Which also means converting an existing stylesheet from CSS to SCSS can be done in stages, as you learn and pick up more of Sass's functionality.

Later, when you've become fluent with Sass (and it won't take long), it really does feel like a natural extension of CSS—as if it's filling holes we all wish were filled by the CSS spec itself. This

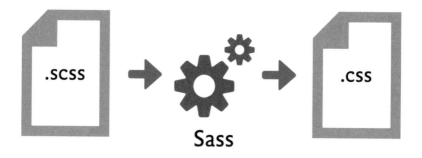

FIG 1: Sass converts its own "power syntax" to plain old CSS.

is why, once I started using Sass, I never once thought it was awkward or laborious—it just feels like CSS should feel. Once you try it, you'll likely stick with it permanently.

Furthermore, Sass is helping CSS get better. By fast-tracking certain features that aren't currently possible without the help of a preprocessor, it's giving CSS authors real-world implementation and feature experimentation. When and if it makes sense, certain Sass functionality could very well inform future CSS specifications.

SASS SYNTAX

There are actually two different syntaxes in Sass. The latest is the aforementioned SCSS syntax. SCSS files use an .scss file extension. This is the syntax I prefer using and advocate for these reasons:

- Since SCSS is a superset of CSS3, I can write CSS as I have for the last ten years and it'll still work just fine.
- It's easy to gradually convert existing stylesheets to use Sass's functionality.
- It doesn't require a shift in code formatting.

A simple SCSS example

Here's an example of how SCSS syntax works. It defines a variable and uses that variable in a CSS declaration.

```scss
$pink: #ea4c89;

p {
  font-size: 12px;
  color: $pink;
}
p strong {
  text-transform: uppercase;
}
```

Which will compile to:

```css
p {
  font-size: 12px;
  color: #ea4c89;
}
p strong {
  text-transform: uppercase;
}
```

That should look very familiar, aside from the $pink variable, and we'll go into variables later in the book. SCSS works around the CSS you already know how to write. And for that, I very much like it.

The original "indented" Sass syntax

The original Sass syntax, on the other hand, is a different animal. Some folks prefer its stripped-down, no-curly-braces-or-semicolons, indented syntax. If you're used to the terseness of programming languages like Ruby or Python, the Sass syntax will look familiar, and you might feel more at home.

Here's the simple example in the original Sass syntax, which will compile exactly the same way as the previous SCSS snippet.

```
$pink: #ea4c89

p
  font-size: 12px
  color: $pink

p strong
  text-transform: uppercase
```

Gone are the braces and semicolons, leaving only whitespace and indents to inform the structure of the declarations. It sure is cleaner and simpler, and some of you may gravitate toward that. It speeds up the initial authoring and cleans up the otherwise noisy code. But for me, I still prefer SCSS, with its closer alignment to normal CSS, for the reasons stated earlier.

The examples in the chapters that follow will use the SCSS syntax. If you prefer the leaner Sass syntax, it's easy to convert. All of the Sass functionality that we'll dive into can be applied to either syntax. It's a matter of preference.

SASS MISCONCEPTIONS

I mentioned earlier that I was reluctant to try Sass. This was partly due to a lot of misconceptions I had prior to using it. Do I need to know Ruby or advanced command-line shenanigans? Will I need to completely change the way I've been writing stylesheets? Will the CSS it outputs be bloated and unreadable?

Thankfully, the answer is "nope" for each of those questions, of course—but I do hear them pop up whenever someone mentions Sass on various internet channels. Let's clear up a few things.

I'm afraid of the command line!

I am by no means a command-line expert, but I've learned a bit here and there over the years—just enough to get me into trouble. I'm not afraid to traverse the file system with it or use Git commands, etc.

That said, I sympathize with designers and front-end developers who don't want to go there. There's a command-line phobia that exists among some folks. For Sass, there's very little command-line action required—in fact, a single command is all you need to grasp. Additionally, there are apps and web frameworks that will obviate the need for the command line. (I'll be introducing those in the next chapter).

So, if you're a command-line avoider, don't let that stop you from trying Sass!

I don't want to change the way I write CSS!

This was the misconception that I suffered from. I'm particular about the way my stylesheets are set up and organized. There's a certain amount of craft that goes into the document. But remember, since the SCSS syntax is a superset of CSS3, you don't have to change anything about the way you write CSS. Commenting, indenting, or not indenting, all your formatting preferences can remain the same when working in .scss files. Once I realized this, I could dive in without fear.

I don't want Sass to change the way I design!

On the flip side, Sass won't solve all of your problems or cure your bad habits. Inefficient, bloated stylesheets can be just as inefficient and bloated when using Sass. Good organization and smart thinking still apply here. In fact, there are instances where Sass can magnify bad practices, and we'll go into that a bit as well. But when used properly and intelligently, Sass can be such a massive assist in creating websites.

Okay. Now that we have the particulars out of the way, let's start having some fun. I think you'll be amazed at what Sass can do. In the next chapter, we'll set up our workflow—how Sass can fit into your process and how easy it is to use the command-line or apps. Let's get Sassing, people.

2
SASS WORKFLOW

NOW THAT we know what Sass is, let's get set up so that we can start using it. Our first task is to install it on your computing device of choice. I mentioned in Chapter 1 that Sass is a program written in Ruby, which translates its native syntax into plain CSS. So, before we start using Sass, we need to install Sass.

INSTALLING SASS ON A MAC

If you're on a Mac (and hooray for you, should you be so lucky), installing Sass couldn't be simpler. Mac OS X comes preinstalled with Ruby, and Sass is packaged as a Ruby "gem," which is a clever programmer term for a Ruby application.

Simply fire up Terminal.app (don't panic!), and at the prompt type the following and hit enter:

```
$ gem install sass
```

That wasn't so bad, right? After you hit enter, you'll see the following results stream by in Terminal:

```
Fetching: sass-3.2.10.gem (100%)
Successfully installed sass-3.2.10
1 gem installed
Installing ri documentation for sass-3.2.10...
Installing RDoc documentation for sass-3.2.10...
```

Congratulations! You've just installed Sass.

At the time of this writing, the latest official version of Sass is 3.2.10, and Terminal is nice enough to relay that bit of info to us.

Installing the latest pre-release version

You can also choose to live on the bleeding edge, and install the latest alpha version by adding a pre flag at the end of the command. Using the latest alpha is not only safe, but it also enables you to take advantage of the latest functionality.

To get the latest and greatest, type this in the terminal prompt and hit enter:

```
$ gem install sass --pre
```

You'll see the results stream by once again, this time confirming the 3.3.0 alpha has been installed.

```
Fetching: sass-3.3.0.alpha.3.gem (100%)
Successfully installed sass-3.3.0.alpha.3
1 gem installed
Installing ri documentation for sass-3.3.0.alpha.3...
Installing RDoc documentation for sass-3.3.0.alpha.3...
```

You're now living on the edge, and I salute your daring leap of faith.

INSTALLING SASS ON WINDOWS

Unlike Mac OS X, Windows doesn't come with Ruby pre-installed. The official Sass website recommends RubyInstaller for Windows to get things running on your PC (http://bkaprt.com/sass/5/). Once Ruby is installed, you'll be able to follow the rest of the commands discussed in this chapter.

TELLING SASS WHICH FILES TO WATCH

Okay. We've installed Sass, so now what? We need to tell Sass which files to "watch." Meaning, while we're editing a stylesheet, we want Sass to monitor that file and convert the .scss file with all our nifty Sass syntax to the browser-ready .css file every time we make changes. There are a few ways to do this:

- A simple command via the command line.
- A desktop app (there are several) that will help you manage your Sass files and their output.

Let's tackle the command-line option first. And fear not! It's simple. Essentially the command tells Sass to watch a specified .scss file, and convert it to a target .css file.

For example:

```
$ sass --watch screen.scss:screen.css
```

After you run the above command, Sass will start monitoring any changes made to screen.scss. You'll see this message in the terminal after hitting return:

```
>>> Sass is watching for changes. Press Ctrl-C to stop.
```

If the file is updated, Sass will convert and overwrite screen.css automagically. In other words, every time you save changes in your Sass document, the CSS file will update instantaneously.

FIG 2.1: A typical directory-organization structure for Sass files.

The file names don't have to match. For instance, this would work just as well (though it might be confusing):

```
$ sass --watch werewolf.scss:vampire.css
```

Furthermore, the files don't have to be in the same directory. In fact, I find it useful to separate my .scss files from my .css files. This isn't a requirement, but it helps keep things organized.

Sass File Organization

FIGURE 2.1 shows a typical setup, with a main stylesheets directory, which contains the Sass-generated .css files and a sass directory that contains all the .scss that I'm working with.

You can also tell Sass to watch an entire directory, rather than just a single stylesheet. So using the above file structure, I could use the following watch command to monitor changes on any of the .scss files in my project (provided I'm currently in the -/ directory that holds my stylesheets and images in the terminal):

```
$ sass --watch stylesheets/sass:stylesheets
```

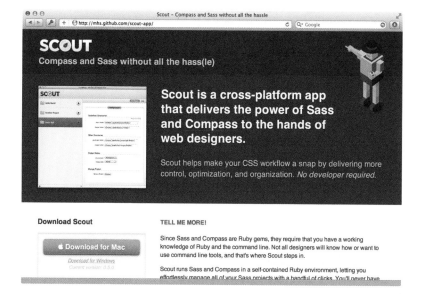

FIG 2.2: The Scout website.

USING APPS INSTEAD OF THE COMMAND LINE

The commands we've gone over so far are extremely simple, and I have faith that you, astute front-end crafter that you are, wouldn't find it difficult to add those bits of typing to your workflow. That said, there are desktop applications that make it even easier to manage the monitoring and output of Sass files. They're worth a look regardless of your comfort level with the command line.

Scout

Scout (http://bkaprt.com/sass/6/) is a free desktop app for both Mac and Windows that provides "a self-contained Ruby environment, letting you effortlessly manage all of your Sass projects with a handful of clicks." In other words, Scout gives you a

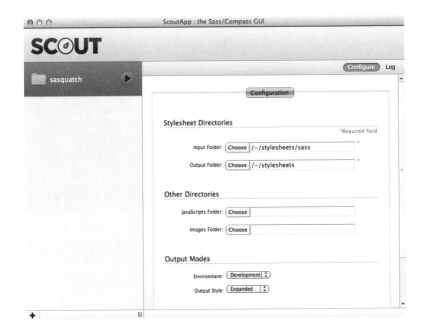

FIG 2.3: Scout's dead simple setup-configuration screen.

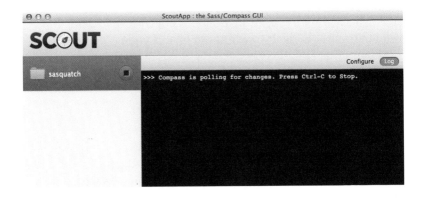

FIG 2.4: As Scout watches your Sass files, the "Log" keeps you updated with its compiling status.

FIG 2.5: The CodeKit website.

nice, visual interface to set up your watched directories and files rather than using the command line (**FIG 2.2-FIG 2.3**).

Once you've chosen input and output folders, simply click the play button for your project and Scout will start monitoring files. The "Log" section will display the terminal updates (**FIG 2.4**).

Scout is a straightforward and convenient way to completely avoid the command line if that's your thing (and to avoid Ruby installation if you're running Windows).

CodeKit

Like Scout, CodeKit (http://bkaprt.com/sass/7/; for Mac OS only) compiles your Sass files with a simple GUI. But it also compiles LESS, Stylus, Haml, CoffeeScript, JavaScript, and others. Additionally, CodeKit has other bells and whistles that optimize

LiveReload 2 proudly presents...

The Web Developer Wonderland

(a happy land where browsers don't need a Refresh button)

CSS edits and image changes apply live.
CoffeeScript, SASS, LESS and others just work.

Citizenship is granted through the Mac App Store.
Windows permanent residency issues are being worked out,
temporary stay already allowed.

What does LiveReload do?

LiveReload monitors changes in the file
system. As soon as you save a file, it is
preprocessed as needed, and the browser
is refreshed.

FIG 2.6: The LiveReload website.

files and images and automatically reload your browser as you
develop (**FIG 2.5**).

LiveReload

LiveReload (http://bkaprt.com/sass/8/) monitors any file changes,
including Sass compiling, as you work and automatically reloads
the browser. It's available for both Mac and Windows (**FIG 2.6**).

Compass.app

Compass.app (http://bkaprt.com/sass/9/) is a little menu bar app
for Mac, Windows, and Linux that watches and compiles Sass
files for you (**FIG 2.7**).

In addition to desktop apps, some development frameworks
have built-in support for Sass. Ruby on Rails, for instance, will

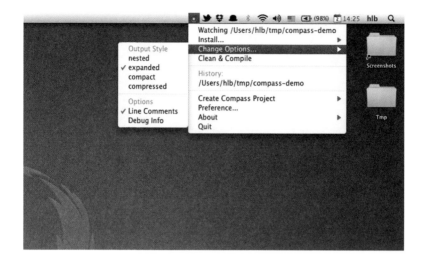

FIG 2.7: Compass.app's menubar options.

auto-compile Sass files into CSS files when the stylesheets are requested. Again, no command line required.

So, you can see there are several options should you find yourself allergic to the command-line, though I hope it's clear that the commands for running Sass are few and uncomplicated.

Now that we have Sass installed and ready to watch files, let's move on and talk about output formatting, commenting, and nesting.

CHOOSING AN OUTPUT STYLE

Like many of you, I learned web design by viewing source. It's an incredible luxury to be able to look under the hood of a website to see how it's put together. For that reason, I've always put a fair amount of care into formatting my markup and stylesheets: the way I indent declarations where the closing brackets go, how I group sections of the stylesheet using whitespace, etc. All of this might seem like unnecessary particularity, but since our CSS is a potential learning tool for others, we're not just creating these files for our own benefit.

With Sass, you're no longer crafting that `.css` file. Instead, you're authoring the `.scss` file that no one sees, and Sass's output of the final might differ from your own formatting preference. It was this (admittedly OCD-ish) formatting control trade-off that initially turned me off and prevented me from using Sass. That may sound ridiculous, but if the stylesheet was a product of my craftsmanship, I very much cared about how it was organized and formatted.

Eventually I got over it—so much so, that I wrote this book. In the end, the formatting differences were nitpicks. The resulting files are still perfectly human-readable. In fact, Sass offers several output styles to choose from, and it's a good time to go over those now.

Nested (the default)

The default style that Sass spits out is nested, which indents each rule to reflect the structure of the HTML it's styling. Here's an example of the nested style:

```
ol {
  margin: 10px 0;
  padding: 10px 0; }
  ol li {
    font-size: 2em;
    line-height: 1.4; }
    ol li p {
      color: #333; }
```

Expanded

The expanded style is a more typical format similar to stylesheets that are crafted by hand. For those viewing source on your amazing CSS, this format will be most familiar.

Here's an example of the expanded style:

```
ol {
  margin: 10px 0;
  padding: 10px 0;
}

ol li {
  font-size: 2em;
  line-height: 1.4;
}

ol li p {
  color: #333;
}
```

Each closing bracket appears on its own line at the end of the declaration. Sass inserts a line break between declarations, which seems unnecessary, but aside from that nitpick, this is the style I like to use in my own projects. It closely resembles the format I use when creating stylesheets by hand without Sass (which is increasingly rare!).

To use this expanded style instead of the default nested style, we just add a flag to the simple command that tells Sass to watch files:

```
$ sass --watch --style expanded screen.scss:screen.css
```

Compact

The compact style puts each declaration on one line, emphasizing the selectors. The idea is you can easily scan the left side to find visually grouped rules, with line breaks between. Personally, I find it difficult to find particular rules, but I've even seen some crazy CSS-ers hand-code their stylesheets in this format because they like the balance between readability and optimization.

Here's an example of the compact style:

```
ol { margin: 10px 0; padding: 10px 0; }
ol li { font-size: 2em; line-height: 1.4; }
ol li p { color: #333; }
```

And here's how you specify the compact style when running the sass command:

```
$ sass --watch --style compact screen.scss:screen.css
```

Compressed

The fourth and final style is compressed, which removes all spaces and line breaks to reduce the stylesheet's file size. It's nearly impossible to read, but that's intentional: the compressed style is meant for efficiency, not humans.

Here's an example:

```
ol{margin:10px 0;padding:10px 0;}ol li{font- »
  size:2em;line-height:1.4;}ol li p{color:#333;}
```

And here's how to specify the compressed style:

```
$ sass --watch --style compressed screen.scss:screen.css
```

Browsers don't need spaces and line breaks, so why not take them out to save space? I'd argue this format isn't conducive to learning from, but for large stylesheets, every byte counts, and it's nice of Sass to include this option.

The compressed style lends itself particularly well to highly-trafficked web apps, in which the performance of every file is crucial. For a personal website this may not matter as much, and a more human-readable style might be a nicer option for those who are looking to learn from your source code.

It's also worth mentioning that with the prevalence of inspector tools built into browsers, the formatting of the .css file matters less today than it did several years ago. Instead of viewing source to dissect a stylesheet, you can inspect a website with browser tools to gain much stronger insight into how the CSS is constructed, and these tools will display the CSS in an easy-to-read format regardless of what the .css file looks like.

Whichever style you choose to output your CSS, it doesn't much matter for your own workflow. Since you'll be living in the .scss file for authoring, you can still do all the personalized formatting you're used to obsessing over. So treat the .scss as your perfectly-crafted document, and let Sass output the results into a stylesheet browsers (and humans) can understand.

DON'T EDIT YOUR OUTPUT!

At this point, it's important to note that when you're using Sass, you'll no longer be editing any .css files. The .scss files are where you'll live and breathe. The reason being, any changes you make to the .css file will eventually get overridden as soon as you update the .scss and Sass compiles the output. So stick to the .scss and blissfully ignore its output.

WE HAVE A WORKFLOW, NOW LET'S WORK

We've talked about how to set up Sass. We've also talked about how to add Sass to your workflow by using either the command line or a third-party app. Finally, we talked about choosing an output style for your Sass-ified CSS. We're now ready to start using Sass, taking advantage of all the time-saving features it injects into our daily work on increasingly complex web projects. Off we go, to Chapter 3...

3 USING SASS

IN THIS CHAPTER, I'll share many of the features I use in Sass every day in my own projects. I've whipped up a fictional project specifically for this book so that we can talk about Sass's functionality in a real-world situation. The project is called Sasquatch Records—a simple website for a record label that focuses on the supernatural musical stylings of mythical, elusive, beasts (FIG 3.1).

The capabilities of Sass are overwhelming—it's a very powerful tool to help bring sanity to creating complex stylesheets. With so many possibilities at our disposal, I'd like to point out the parts of Sass I see as most valuable to the web designer, and also the easiest to add to your workflow.

NESTING RULES

With Sass, you can nest CSS rules inside each other instead of repeating selectors in separate declarations. The nesting also reflects the markup structure.

Sasquatch Records

HOME BANDS SHOWS STORE

LATEST NEWS

New Artist: Loch Nestle
OCTOBER 31, 2012

They call Los Angeles the City of Angels. I didn't find it to be that exactly, but I'll allow as there are some nice folks there. 'Course, **I can't say I seen London**, and I never been to France, and I ain't never seen no queen in her damn undies as the fella says. But I'll tell you what, after seeing Los Angeles and thisahere story I'm about to unfold —wal, I guess I seen somethin' ever' bit as stupefyin' as ya'd see in any a those other places, and in English too, so I can die with a smile on my face without feelin' like the good Lord gypped me.

These men are nihilists, Donny, nothing to be afraid of. Ac magna justo pellentesque ac lectus quis elit blandit fringilla a ut turpis praesent. Any further harm visited upon Bunny, **shall be visited tenfold** upon your head. Felis ligula, malesuada suscipit malesuada non, ultrices non urna sed orci ipsum, placerat id. Condimentum rutrum, rhoncus ac lorem aliquam placerat posuere neque, at dignissim magna ullamcorper in. Ever hear of the Seattle Seven?

POPULAR VIDEOS

 This is the title
Lorem ipsum dolor sit amet, consectetur adipisicing elit. Lorem ipsum dolor sit amet.
AUGUST 10, 2011

 This is the title
Lorem ipsum dolor sit amet, consectetur adipisicing elit. Lorem ipsum dolor sit amet.
AUGUST 10, 2011

 This is the title
Lorem ipsum dolor sit amet, consectetur adipisicing elit. Lorem ipsum dolor sit amet.
AUGUST 10, 2011

FOLLOW US

 Dribbble

Flickr

Facebook

FIG 3.1: Sasquatch Records, a fictional website I'll be using to showcase some Sass examples.

For example, the main portion of the Sasquatch Records header's markup is structured like so:

```
<header role="banner">
  <div id="logo">
    <img src="logo.png" alt="Sasquatch Records" />
  </div>

  <h1>Sasquatch Records</h1>
  ...
</header>
```

When writing the SCSS, I can mirror that element nesting, letting Sass build the full selectors. I personally like to put a blank line before nested selectors to set them off from the CSS properties that share that same nesting level:

```scss
header[role="banner"] {
  margin: 20px 0 30px 0;
  border-bottom: 4px solid #333;

  #logo {
    float: left;
    margin: 0 20px 0 0;

    img {
      display: block;
      opacity: .95;
    }
  }

  h1 {
    padding: 15px 0;
    font-size: 54px;
    line-height: 1;
    font-family: Jubilat, Georgia, serif;
    font-weight: bold;
  }
}
```

Which will compile into:

```css
header[role="banner"] {
  margin: 20px 0 30px 0;
  border-bottom: 4px solid #333;
}
header[role="banner"] #logo {
  float: left;
  margin: 0 20px 0 0;
}
header[role="banner"] #logo img {
  display: block;
  opacity: .95;
}
header[role="banner"] h1 {
  padding: 15px 0;
```

```
  font-size: 54px;
  line-height: 1;
  font-family: Jubilat, Georgia, serif;
  font-weight: bold;
}
```

Instead of repeating each element in the selector, Sass simplifies things by nesting to show hierarchy. Do be careful when nesting, of course. Sometimes you don't need to be so verbose with the selectors, and excessive nesting can actually hinder readability. A few levels deep works great, and for module-specific declarations, like the example above, Sass's nesting is a big time-saver.

NESTING NAMESPACED PROPERTIES

In addition to nesting rules, you can nest properties that share a namespace in Sass (e.g., `font-family`, `font-size`, `font-weight`, etc.) like so:

```
header[role="banner"] h1 {
  padding: 15px 0;
  font: {
    size: 54px;
    family: Jubilat, Georgia, serif;
    weight: bold;
  }
  line-height: 1;
}
```

That'll compile to:

```
header[role="banner"] h1 {
  padding: 15px 0;
  font-size: 54px;
  font-family: Jubilat, Georgia, serif;
  font-weight: bold;
  line-height: 1;
}
```

Similarly, there are many properties in the text- namespace. We can use Sass nesting to save some retyping:

```
text: {
  transform: uppercase;
  decoration: underline;
  align: center;
}
```

And background- is another good example:

```
background: {
  color: #ea4c89;
  size: 16px 16px;
  image: url(sasquatch.png);
  repeat: no-repeat;
  position: top left;
}
```

Nesting in Sass means less typing, using indentation to reflect the selector (and property) formation. It's also a concept that's easy to grasp for anyone writing CSS—not a huge mental leap.

REFERENCING PARENT SELECTORS WITH &

Along with nesting rules and properties, Sass adds the ability to reference the current parent selector using the ampersand as a special placeholder.

For example, within a declaration for links, we can add hover styles that override their color and border color:

```
a {
  font-weight: bold;
  text-decoration: none;
  color: red;
  border-bottom: 2px solid red;
```

```
  &:hover {
    color: maroon;
    border-color: maroon;
  }
}
```

The ampersand inserts the parent selector, in this case a, which will compile like so:

```
a {
  font-weight: bold;
  text-decoration: none;
  color: red;
  border-bottom: 2px solid red;
}
a:hover {
  color: maroon;
  border-color: maroon;
}
```

Here's another example of using the ampersand to reference the parent selector, in which different classes trigger different styles:

```
li a {
  color: blue;

  &.alert {
    color: red;
  }

  &.success {
    color: green;
  }
}
```

Which will compile to:

```
li a {
  color: blue;
}
li a.alert {
  color: red;
}
li a.success {
  color: green;
}
```

The ampersand is also useful in inserting overrides that happen in the presence of a specific class. For example, let's say we style paragraphs in the main section of the site, but we want a slightly different style on a specific page. We add a class to the body, and then we can use the ampersand to slip this overriding declaration into the main one:

```
section.main p {
  margin: 0 0 20px 0;
  font-size: 18px;
  line-height: 1.5;

  body.store & {
    font-size: 16px;
    line-height: 1.4;
  }
}
```

Which will compile to:

```
section.main p {
  margin: 0 0 20px 0;
  font-size: 18px;
  line-height: 1.5;
}
body.store section.main p {
  font-size: 16px;
  line-height: 1.4;
}
```

On store pages (or those with `<body class="store">`), paragraphs will have slightly smaller type. But instead of writing an entirely new declaration, we've nested it, using the ampersand to create a unique case and letting Sass reconstruct the full selector. Again, this is time-saving stuff, while keeping related rules in one group.

COMMENTING IN SASS

For comments within the stylesheet, Sass supports single-line comments in addition to the standard, multi-line comments in CSS.

For example:

```
/* This is a multi-line comment that will
appear in the final .css file. */
```

You can ensure important comments (copyright info, attribution, notes on hacks, etc.) appear in the compressed style output by inserting an ! as the first character of the comment:

```
/*! This is a multi-line comment that will
appear in the final .css file. Even in compressed style.
*/
```

Single-line comments use the // prefix at the beginning of each line and aren't included in the final output, so you can safely use them for private comments:

```
// This is a single-line comment.
// Single-line comments are removed from the .css file.
// So you can say whatever you'd like here.
// Confession: I genuinely enjoy listening to ABBA.
// And Hall & Oates.
```

In addition to hiding your questionable taste in music, single-line comments are great for documenting your SCSS for internal team development. Commenting can be frequent and detailed without the worry of adding extraneous bloat to the CSS output.

VARIABLES

Sass is full of incredibly helpful features that make our lives as front-end crafters easier. But if I could choose only one of those features as the most helpful, it'd be variables.

We repeat ourselves so often in a stylesheet. Colors, fonts, background images, widths, etc.—there are patterns that require an epic battle with find-and-replace should any of those patterns be changed. Variables make all of that much simpler and easier to maintain.

Variables in Sass are defined like regular CSS rules using the $ like so:

```
$color-main: #333;
$color-light: #999;
$color-accent: #ea4c89;

$font-sans: "Proxima Nova", "Helvetica Neue", »
  Helvetica, Arial, sans-serif;
$font-serif: Jubilat, Georgia, serif;
```

Once defined, they can be invoked within declarations:

```
body {
  padding: 0 8%;
  font-family: $font-sans;
  font-size: 100%;
  color: $color-main;
  background: #fff url(../img/bg.jpg) repeat-x -80% 0;
}
```

Sass will replace the variables with their values in the CSS output:

```
body {
  padding: 0 8%;
  font-family: "Proxima Nova", "Helvetica Neue", »
    Helvetica, Arial, sans-serif;
  font-size: 100%;
  color: #333;
  background: #fff url(../img/bg.jpg) repeat-x -80% 0;
}
```

With Sass variables, wholesale changes to a stylesheet's re-peated patterns are updated in seconds, so you don't need to hunt through the entire file. Hooray!

Using variables for style guides

Jina Bolton wrote a great article on how Sass variables can help with creating a style guide from a brand palette (http://bkaprt. com/sass/10/). Says Jina:

> To keep our style guide relevant, it lives in our internal-only admin section on the very same application it describes. We display our color palette alongside the relevant Sass variables and since we've built the style guide into the application using the same front-end, we can use the same variables we're referencing to render this palette. When we change values to these variables, the palette updates automatically (**FIG 3.2**).

Rather than creating a static style guide that can become outdated and irrelevant, using Sass variables to define a brand's palette means everyone can help keep the style guide up to date and maintainable.

Using the style guide's variables as a foundation, Jina goes on to talk about tapping into Sass's color functions to create varia-tions within the brand palette.

For example, here's the tiny color palette for the Sasquatch Records site, using single-line comments to note each color since it's not crucial to the CSS output:

$color-background	
$color-background-alt	
$color-background-alt2	
$color-text	
$color-text-alt	
$color-text-alert	
$color-text-callout	
$color-border	

FIG 3.2: Jina Bolton uses Sass to help create style guides.

```
$color-main:   #333;      // black
$color-light:  #999;      // grey
$color-accent: #ea4c89;   // pink
```

Next, using the darken or lighten color function in Sass, we can generate different shades of color that will always be based on the brand palette.

Let's darken the pink (#ea4c89) by 30%:

```
section.secondary {
    background: darken($color-accent, 30%);
}
```

When compiled, Sass will calculate the color by darkening the original pink by 30% and referencing the hex color equivalent:

```
section.secondary {
    background: #8d1040;
}
```

We can also lighten colors:

```
section.secondary {
  background: lighten($color-accent, 30%);
}
```

Which will compile to:

```
section.secondary {
  background: #fad5e3;
}
```

What about CSS variables?

One of the terrific things about Sass (and CSS preprocessors in general) is that it provides a testing ground for features that might join the ranks of a proposed standard. In other words, Sass can move at a quicker pace, implementing features that don't yet exist in the CSS spec. If these prove successful enough, they could be folded into the standard.

Variables are a good example of this, and are probably the most used feature of CSS preprocessors. The groundswell of support for including variables as an official CSS feature has been magnified by the use of Sass and LESS. Currently a W3C working draft, "CSS Variables Module Level 1," is being developed (http://bkaprt.com/sass/11/), and the latest WebKit nightly builds have implemented support for variables. That means native support for CSS variables is on its way.

Unfortunately, at the time of this writing, the CSS variable syntax differs from that of Sass, and is not as elegant or simple to grasp. For example, here is how you define a CSS variable for the root element of the document:

```
:root {
  var-color-main: #333;
}
```

And here is how you would use the variable within a declaration:

```
#main p {
  color: var(color-main);
}
```

The proposal uses a `var` prefix to define the variable but a `var(variable-name)` syntax for values. It's a bit clumsy and confusing, but this is a work in progress, and many are clamoring for the Sass-like `$foo` syntax in both types of use. Here's hoping it eventually works out this way.

Most important, with browser support limited to bleeding-edge versions of WebKit, CSS variables aren't usable in production anyway—yet another reason to stick to Sass.

MIXINS

Let's move on to my second favorite Sass feature: mixins. Where variables let you define and reuse values throughout the stylesheet, mixins allow you to define and reuse blocks of styles. Rather than typing the same rules over and over again in various declarations, you can use mixins to define a group of styles just once and refer to it anytime those styles are needed.

To illustrate, let's create a mixin for a heading style that I'm using in a few areas on the Sasquatch Records site (**FIG 3.3**). While these titles may appear in various locations on the page, their CSS is identical, which is a perfect situation for a mixin.

First, we'll define a mixin in Sass using the `@mixin` directive at the top of the `.scss` file. I'll name it `title-style`, and I'll define the rules for margins and fonts:

```
@mixin title-style {
  margin: 0 0 20px 0;
  font-family: $font-serif;
  font-size: 20px;
  font-weight: bold;
  text-transform: uppercase;
}
```

Once it's defined, we can now refer to this mixin anywhere we'd like to insert those styles by using the @include directive.

On the Sasquatch site, we have a section of the stylesheet that defines rules for the page's main section, and we want the mixin to style all <h2> elements:

```
section.main h2 {
  @include title-style;
}
```

This will compile to:

```
section.main h2 {
  margin: 0 0 20px 0;
  font-family: Jubilat, Georgia, serif;
  font-size: 20px;
  font-weight: bold;
  text-transform: uppercase;
}
```

But we also want to style <h3> elements in the sidebar the exact same way. So, later in the stylesheet we can call the same mixin, which will compile the same rules:

```
section.secondary h3 {
  @include title-style;
}
```

This lets us avoid duplicating the shared styles—or adding a class to the markup that both headings could theoretically share.

Mixins can be included with additional rules as well:

```
section.secondary h3 {
  @include title-style;
  color: #999;
}
```

Which will compile to:

```
section.secondary h3 {
  margin: 0 0 20px 0;
  font-family: Jubilat, Georgia, serif;
  font-size: 20px;
  font-weight: bold;
  text-transform: uppercase;
  color: #999;
}
```

Shared styles can be abstracted into mixins, and you'll still have the ability to override or augment those styles with additional rules. Powerful stuff!

Mixin arguments

Sass mixins can also take arguments that we pass to the mixin when we call it. For example, let's add an argument for specifying a color along with our title-style mixin.

Specify arguments with variables inside parentheses when defining the mixin:

```
@mixin title-style($color) {
  margin: 0 0 20px 0;
  font-family: $font-serif;
  font-size: 20px;
  font-weight: bold;
  text-transform: uppercase;
  color: $color;
}
```

When calling the mixin, we can now pass a color to it (here a lovely burnt orange), along with the other rules:

```
section.main h2 {
  @include title-style(#c63);
}
```

Which will compile to:

```
section.main h2 {
  margin: 0 0 20px 0;
  font-family: Jubilat, Georgia, serif;
  font-size: 20px;
  font-weight: bold;
  text-transform: uppercase;
  color: #c63;
}
```

Multiple arguments

You can pass multiple arguments by separating the values with commas in the mixin definition:

```
@mixin title-style($color, $background) {
  margin: 0 0 20px 0;
  font-family: $font-serif;
  font-size: 20px;
  font-weight: bold;
  text-transform: uppercase;
  color: $color;
  background: $background;
}
```

And here's the mixin being called from two different selectors, passing differing arguments for color and background:

```
section.main h2 {
  @include title-style(#c63, #eee);
}
```

```
section.secondary·h3 {
  @include title-style(#39c, #333);
}
```

Which in this case will compile to:

```
section.main h2 {
  margin: 0 0 20px 0;
  font-family: Jubilat, Georgia, serif;
  font-size: 20px;
  font-weight: bold;
  text-transform: uppercase;
  color: #c63;
  background: #eee;
}
section.secondary h3 {
  margin: 0 0 20px 0;
  font-family: Jubilat, Georgia, serif;
  font-size: 20px;
  font-weight: bold;
  text-transform: uppercase;
  color: #39c;
  background: #333;
}
```

You can start to see how flexible mixins can be. Through arguments, consistently-shared rules can sit alongside those that differ slightly.

Defining defaults for arguments

When you use mixin arguments, it's often convenient to define defaults. That way, you simply call the mixin with no arguments, if that's the norm, but can still pass in overrides.

```
@mixin title-style($color, $background: #eee) {
  margin: 0 0 20px 0;
  font-family: $font-serif;
```

```
  font-size: 20px;
  font-weight: bold;
  text-transform: uppercase;
  color: $color;
  background: $background;
}
```

Even though we've defined a light gray default for the mixin's background, we can pass an argument for something different:

```
section.main h2 {
  @include title-style(#c63);
}
section.secondary h3 {
  @include title-style(#39c, #333);
}
```

Which will again compile to:

```
section.main h2 {
  margin: 0 0 20px 0;
  font-family: Jubilat, Georgia, serif;
  font-size: 20px;
  font-weight: bold;
  text-transform: uppercase;
  color: #c63;
  background: #eee;
}
section.secondary h3 {
  margin: 0 0 20px 0;
  font-family: Jubilat, Georgia, serif;
  font-size: 20px;
  font-weight: bold;
  text-transform: uppercase;
  color: #39c;
  background: #333;
}
```

Additionally, when you have multiple, default arguments defined for a mixin, you can override those selectively without having to redefine them all.

For example, let's say our mixin defined values for both `$color` and `$background`:

```scss
@mixin title-style($color: blue, $background: green) {
  margin: 0 0 20px 0;
  font-family: $font-serif;
  font-size: 20px;
  font-weight: bold;
  text-transform: uppercase;
  color: $color;
  background: $background;
}
```

And if we want the color to be the default blue, but we want to override the background to be pink, we only need to pass the background:

```scss
section.main h2 {
  @include title-style($background: pink);
}
```

Which will compile to:

```scss
section.main h2 {
  margin: 0 0 20px 0;
  font-family: Jubilat, Georgia, serif;
  font-size: 20px;
  font-weight: bold;
  text-transform: uppercase;
  color: blue;
  background: pink;
}
```

A nice time-saver, which keeps those arguments defined in one place (the mixin).

CSS3 LOVES MIXINS

The use of mixins with arguments really shines in CSS3, where we often repeat vendor-prefixed rules throughout the stylesheet to achieve rounded corners, drop shadows, gradients, transitions, etc. While the values might differ for these properties throughout the design, so much is shared and repeated, and Sass makes dealing with CSS3 "stacks" an absolute breeze. Can't remember the syntax for creating CSS gradients? Make it a mixin!

border-radius

Here's a mixin for handling CSS3 rounded corners in all browsers, with an argument for the radius value:

```
@mixin rounded($radius) {
  -webkit-border-radius: $radius;
    -moz-border-radius: $radius;
        border-radius: $radius;
}
```

We can then make anything on the page rounded by calling that mixin:

```
ol.slats li a img {
  float: left;
  margin: 0 10px 0 0;
  padding: 4px;
  border: 1px solid #ddd;
  @include rounded(3px);
}
div.module {
  padding: 20px;
  background: #eee;
  @include rounded(10px);
}
```

Which will compile to:

```
ol.slats li a img {
  float: left;
  margin: 0 10px 0 0;
  padding: 4px;
  border: 1px solid #ddd;
  -webkit-border-radius: 3px;
    -moz-border-radius: 3px;
        border-radius: 3px;
}
div.module {
  padding: 20px;
  background: #eee;
  -webkit-border-radius: 10px;
    -moz-border-radius: 10px;
        border-radius: 10px;
}
```

box-shadow

Here's another example using multiple arguments: a mixin for creating drop shadows in CSS3 that gives us the ability to pass in values for the vertical and horizontal positions of the shadow, the amount of blur, and the color:

```
@mixin shadow($x, $y, $blur, $color) {
  -webkit-box-shadow: $x $y $blur $color;
    -moz-box-shadow: $x $y $blur $color;
        box-shadow: $x $y $blur $color;
}
```

Let's add this mixin to the previous div.module example, making the shadow appear straight from the top, down 1px, with 2px of blur, and black at 50% opacity:

```
div.module {
  padding: 20px;
  background: #eee;
  @include rounded(10px);
  @include shadow(0, 1px, 2px, rgba(0,0,0,.5));
}
```

Which will compile to:

```
div.module {
  padding: 20px;
  background: #eee;
  -webkit-border-radius: 10px;
     -moz-border-radius: 10px;
          border-radius: 10px;
    -webkit-box-shadow: 0, 1px, 2px, rgba(0,0,0,.5);
       -moz-box-shadow: 0, 1px, 2px, rgba(0,0,0,.5);
            box-shadow: 0, 1px, 2px, rgba(0,0,0,.5);
}
```

No need to write those vendor-prefix stacks over and over. Write once, reuse whenever you'd like.

CSS3 gradients

CSS3 gradient syntax is ugly. It differs depending on the browser, it's not easy to remember, and historically the spec has evolved quite a bit, forcing authors to update their stylesheets. For all of these reasons, Sass (and specifically the mixin) makes using CSS3 gradients bearable and future-proof. Should the spec change again, we'll only need to update the syntax once, in the mixin.

For example, let's add a CSS linear gradient to the active tab style on the Sasquatch Records design (FIG 3.4). To ensure the gradient works in the most browsers possible and falls back to a solid color should the browser not support CSS gradients, we'll need a hefty stack of properties:

```
header nav[role="navigation"] ul li.active a {
  padding: 3px 8px;
  color: #fff;
  -webkit-border-radius: 4px;
    -moz-border-radius: 4px;
        border-radius: 4px;
  /* Fallback for sad browsers */
  background-color: #d42a78;
  /* Mozilla Firefox */
  background-image: -moz-linear-gradient(#ff70b1, »
    #d42a78);
  /* Opera */
  background-image: -o-linear-gradient(#ff70b1, »
    #d42a78);
  /* WebKit (Safari/Chrome 10) */
  background-image: -webkit-gradient(linear, left top, »
    left bottom, color-stop(0, #ff70b1), color-stop(1, »
    #d42a78));
  /* WebKit (Chrome 11+) */
  background-image: -webkit-linear-gradient(#ff70b1, »
    #d42a78);
  /* IE10 */
  background-image: -ms-linear-gradient(#ff70b1, »
    #d42a78);
  /* W3C */
  background-image: linear-gradient(#ff70b1, #d42a78);
}
```

Notice each vendor-prefixed property takes the same "from" and "to" hex colors to create the gradient going from top to bottom. Using a Sass mixin, we can make this much simpler to call by plugging in the gradient's colors as variables passed to the mixin. Who can remember all of these variations each time a gradient is needed? Let's make this easier on ourselves.

First, let's build a mixin called linear-gradient, taking out the hex colors so that we can pass those in as $from and $to variables throughout the stylesheet using whatever hues we'd like.

Sasquat

HOME   BANDS

ᴦ NEWS

FIG: 3.4: Shared heading styles on the Sasquatch Records site.

```
@mixin linear-gradient($from, $to) {
  /* Fallback for sad browsers */
  background-color: $to;
  /* Mozilla Firefox */
  background-image:    -moz-linear-gradient($from, $to);
  /* Opera */
  background-image:      -o-linear-gradient($from, $to);
  /* WebKit (Safari 4+, Chrome 1+) */
  background-image:       -webkit-gradient(linear, »
    left top, left bottom, color-stop(0, $from), »
    color-stop(1, $to));
  /* WebKit (Chrome 11+) */
  background-image: -webkit-linear-gradient($from, $to);
  /* IE10 */
  background-image:      -ms-linear-gradient($from, $to);
  /* W3C */
  background-image:          linear-gradient($from, $to);
}
```

Notice that I'm using the $to color to specify the background-color fallback for browsers that don't support CSS gradients.

Thankfully, we only have to write this monstrosity once. Now, when we want to create a simple linear gradient, we just call the mixin with two colors of our choosing and Sass does the rest. For the Sasquatch site, the declaration for the active tab style goes like this:

```
&.active a {
  padding: 3px 8px;
  color: #fff;
  @include rounded(4px);
  @include linear-gradient(#ff70b1, #d42a78);
}
```

That is not only bearable, it just makes sense! As if it's written in English. And I can reuse this pattern, for say a blue button (**FIG 3.5**), on a different selector in the stylesheet without recalling all that gradient syntax garbage:

```
button {
  padding: 5px 10px;
  color: #fff;
  @include rounded(6px);
  @include linear-gradient(#42b3e2, #1a6798);
}
```

As you may know, the linear gradient we're using here is one simple example, and CSS gradients are capable of much more complexity, like color stops, radial gradients, multiple directions, etc. Sass can help with those situations as well, abstracting any shared patterns into a reusable mixin.

CREATING A MIXIN LIBRARY

Mixins are wonderful because they can be written once and used throughout the stylesheet. But often these mixins are even repeated across projects. You'll likely find yourself writing mixins for common CSS3 properties like box-shadow, gradients, CSS

transitions, and patterns like self-clearing floats, `box-sizing`, form elements, etc. Wouldn't it be efficient to also write all of these once and reuse them for any project where you're using Sass?

@import

Enter the `@import` rule, which Sass extends to allow the importing of multiple SCSS files, merging them into a single CSS file when compiled. This is handy for a variety of reasons:

- A single CSS means fewer HTTP connections. Performance!
- Variables can be defined in their own file, then imported whenever needed, regardless of layout and other page-specific styles.
- Imported SCSS files can contain project-agnostic mixins that can be shared and reused.

Here's how `@import` works in practice.

I have a `mixins.scss` file that's imported to all my projects. In that file I've defined some common patterns I'll use in every project. Here's an example of what's inside `mixins.scss`:

```scss
@mixin rounded($radius) {
  -webkit-border-radius: $radius;
     -moz-border-radius: $radius;
          border-radius: $radius;
}
@mixin shadow($x, $y, $blur, $color) {
  -webkit-box-shadow: $x $y $blur $color;
     -moz-box-shadow: $x $y $blur $color;
          box-shadow: $x $y $blur $color;
}
@mixin shadow-inset($x, $y, $blur, $color) {
  -webkit-box-shadow: inset $x $y $blur $color;
     -moz-box-shadow: inset $x $y $blur $color;
          box-shadow: inset $x $y $blur $color;
}
@mixin transition($property) {
  -webkit-transition: $property .2s ease;
     -moz-transition: $property .2s ease;
       -o-transition: $property .2s ease;
          transition: $property .2s ease;
}
@mixin box-sizing {
  -webkit-box-sizing: border-box;
     -moz-box-sizing: border-box;
          box-sizing: border-box;
}
@mixin linear-gradient($from, $to) {
  /* Fallback for sad browsers */
  background-color: $to;
  /* Mozilla Firefox */
  background-image:    -moz-linear-gradient($from, $to);
  /* Opera */
  background-image:      -o-linear-gradient($from, $to);
  /* WebKit (Chrome 11+) */
  background-image:         -webkit-gradient(linear, »
    left top, left bottom, color-stop(0, $from), »
    color-stop(1, $to));
  /* WebKit (Safari 5.1+, Chrome 10+) */
  background-image: -webkit-linear-gradient($from, $to);
```

```
/* IE10 */
background-image:      -ms-linear-gradient($from, $to);
/* W3C */
background-image:         linear-gradient($from, $to);
}
```

At the top of my main stylesheet (screen.scss in this case) where I define all of my layout and other site-specific styles, I use the @import rule to pull those in so that the mixins are available. I also import a reset stylesheet that's reused in every project (again saving on HTTP connections and avoiding copying and pasting the same code) as well as a variables file where I keep variables for site colors, fonts, etc. (**FIG 3.6**). That allows me to import those same variables in other stylesheets—for example, in other pages or sections of the same project, where the style guide applies—without also importing the rest of the layout.

```
// Import other files

@import "reset.scss";
@import "variables.scss";
@import "mixins.scss";

// Site-specific styles

.foo {
  ...
}
```

When Sass compiles the screen.css file, it'll include everything needed from those @import-ed files. So, you have the benefits of a single file download, with the flexibility of multiple files that contain reusable code.

The Compass framework

With mixins, variable files, and @import, you can build your own mighty CSS frameworks to save an immense amount of time when starting new projects. Having complex CSS3 stacks and

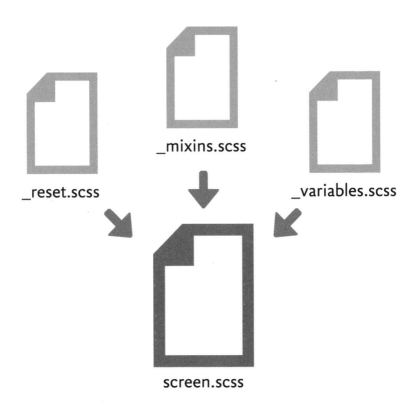

_mixins.scss

_reset.scss

_variables.scss

screen.scss

FIG 3.6: Use @import to merge chunks of your SCSS into one file.

other oft-repeated patterns at your fingertips with just a line of code means more time creating and less time wrangling code.

Taking that organizational advantage to the next level is Compass (http://bkaprt.com/sass/12/), an open-source stylesheet framework built on Sass by Chris Eppstein (a Sass core member and all-around good guy). Compass offers many pre-written CSS patterns, which will be updated as the properties evolve and vendor prefixes can be stripped away. Compass also makes image sprites and typographic systems easier to handle (**FIG 3.7**).

FIG 3.7: The Compass website.

I always suggest creating your own frameworks, as it's best to understand what is happening with your code as much as possible. But as a learning experience, other frameworks can be incredibly beneficial—they let you see how others set up projects and increase their efficiency. And Compass is no exception.

The Bourbon library

The folks at design/development shop thoughtbot have put together an extensive mixin library, called Bourbon (http:// bkaprt.com/sass/13/)—which, coincidentally, I've been drinking too much of, with vermouth and bitters and muddled sugar and fruit (**FIG 3.8**).

A little Googling will unearth many helpful Sassers sharing their mixins on GitHub or their own sites. Chances are, that

FIG 3.8: The Bourbon website.

CSS3 stack that looks ugly and unmaintainable already has a mixin written for it, so take advantage of the community!

@extend

Ever find yourself writing a CSS class that has the same styles as another class, except for just a few other rules?

Here's an example. You have an alert message style with two options at the top of the page. One style handles standard alerts (**FIG 3.9**), while the second style handles positive alerts (**FIG 3.10**). These styles are almost identical, save for the background color.

Typically, we might create a base class for normal alerts and then a second class that overrides the background color only.

```
<h2 class="alert alert-positive">This is a positive »
    alert!</h2>
```

With the styles for each alert set up like so:

Sasquatch Records

HOME   BANDS   SHOWS   STORE

LATEST NEWS

New Artist: Loch Nestle
OCTOBER 31, 2012

They call Los Angeles the City of Angels. I didn't find it to be

POPULAR VIDEOS

 This is the title
Lorem ipsum dolor sit amet,
consectetur adipisicing elit. Lorem
ipsum dolor sit amet.

 Sasquatch Records

HOME   BANDS   SHOWS   STORE

LATEST NEWS

New Artist: Loch Nestle
OCTOBER 31, 2012

They call Los Angeles the City of Angels. I didn't find it to be

POPULAR VIDEOS

 This is the title
Lorem ipsum dolor sit amet,
consectetur adipisicing elit. Lorem
ipsum dolor sit amet.

FIG 3.9-3.10: Two alert styles on the Sasquatch Records site.

```scss
.alert {
  padding: 15px;
  font-size: 1.2em;
  font-weight: normal;
  text-transform: uppercase;
  line-height: 1;
  letter-spacing: 3px;
  text-align: center;
  color: #fff;
  background: $color-accent;
  @include shadow(0, 1px, 2px, rgba(0,0,0,.5));
  @include rounded(10px);
}
.alert-positive {
  background: #9c3;
}
```

Instead of littering the markup with extra classes to handle those small exceptions, we can use Sass's @extend function to "chain together" styles that are shared amongst multiple selectors. Additionally, we can then add extra overriding rules to make a new unique style without duplicating the shared styles.

So if we wanted to use @extend to handle the two types of alert messages, we could simplify the markup to just one class:

```
<h2 class="alert-positive">This is a positive alert! »
  </h2>
```

Then use @extend to include the styles from the h2.alert class, plus the background-color exception:

```
.alert-positive {
  @extend .alert;
  background: #9c3;
}
```

Sass will then efficiently compile the extended class like this:

```
.alert, .alert-positive {
  padding: 15px;
  font-size: 1.2em;
  font-weight: normal;
  text-transform: uppercase;
  line-height: 1;
  letter-spacing: 3px;
  text-align: center;
  color: #fff;
  background: #ea4c89;
      -webkit-box-shadow: 0 1px 2px rgba(0, 0, 0, 0.5);
         -moz-box-shadow: 0 1px 2px rgba(0, 0, 0, 0.5);
              box-shadow: 0 1px 2px rgba(0, 0, 0, 0.5);
    -webkit-border-radius: 10px;
       -moz-border-radius: 10px;
            border-radius: 10px;
}
```

```
.alert-positive {
  background: #9c3;
}
```

Now, sure, we could've written our CSS this way from the beginning, but the @extend syntax makes it faster—not to mention it's clearer which styles are shared between classes. It's far easier to wrap your head around what's happening.

Using @extend also allows us to be terser in our semantics, defining class names based on meaning rather than appearance.

Multiple @extends

You can also @extend multiple classes within a declaration, which chains together all the styles from each class:

```
.alert {
  padding: 15px;
  font-size: 1.2em;
  text-align: center;
  background: $color-accent;
}
.important {
  font-size: 4em;
}
.alert-positive {
  @extend .alert;
  @extend .important;
  background: #9c3;
}
```

Which will compile to:

```
.alert, alert-positive {
  padding: 15px;
  font-size: 1.2em;
  text-align: center;
  background: #ea4c89;
}
```

```
.important, .alert-positive {
  font-size: 4em;
}
.alert-positive {
  background: #9c3;
}
```

Again, Sass efficiently organizes things, grouping the shared styles together using comma-separated selectors and then creating single declarations for any exceptions.

Using placeholder selectors with @extend

What if the class you're extending exists solely for the purpose of extending other styles? In other words, you might create a class that's not used on its own.

Enter placeholder selectors, which allow you to define "phantom" classes that won't appear in the outputted CSS on their own. You can reference placeholders using @extend.

Let's take a look at this in practice. We'll create a class for a block of styles that define a button. We'll use a placeholder selector, which in Sass means prefixing the class name with a % instead of a period.

```
%button {
  padding: 10px;
  font-weight: bold;
  background: blue;
  border-radius: 6px;
}
```

We can call this rule set in other classes as we did previously, using @extend.

```
.buy {
  @extend %button;
}
```

```
.submit {
  @extend %button;
  background: green;
}
```

Sass will compile this like an extended class, but the %button placeholder rule set won't appear in the output:

```
.buy, .submit {
  padding: 10px;
  font-weight: bold;
  background: blue;
  border-radius: 6px;
}
.submit {
  background: green;
}
```

Placeholder selectors are especially helpful in creating blocks of styles for design patterns that may or may not be used (in frameworks, style guides, or starter templates, for example), since unused placeholder classes won't litter the compiled stylesheet.

@extend versus @mixin

Where a mixin will write the same rules in each declaration it's called from, @extend will create multiple, comma-separated selectors for shared styles. It's good to keep that difference in mind when you're debating which to use.

For example, overuse of a mixin can result in a bloated CSS file in which the contents of the mixin are present in the compiled CSS every time it's called in Sass. If you find yourself using a mixin over and over throughout the stylesheet, keep in mind how that will compile, and consider whether it makes sense to use @extend or turn those repeated styles into a class that gets reused in the markup instead.

Don't over @extend yourself

Using @extend is a powerful way to share styles between classes, but be careful; when used too much, the compiled CSS starts to get a bit hairy. Extending the same class repeatedly throughout the stylesheet can result in a monster declaration. When using Sass, it's easy to forget what the compiled stylesheet will ultimately look like—make sure to keep tabs on how Sass outputs your work.

Okay. You now have the power! We've covered the basics of Sass: how to set it up, how the syntax works, how it can fit neatly beside your current coding habits, and how to use the core features through nesting, variables, mixins, and @extend.

Sass is capable of even more, if you want to dive deeper. In the next chapter, we're going to talk about how Sass can help with responsive design and media queries. Let's take the plunge.

4 SASS AND MEDIA QUERIES

I wanted the main focus of this book to be the basics of Sass, proving that Sass doesn't have to mean ripping apart your workflow. But in this final chapter, I do want to talk about some advanced techniques with Sass and media queries that have greatly simplified some otherwise complex CSS in my daily work.

Sass is as powerful as you want it to be. Using it for variables and a few mixins will make your life easier. But it can go beyond that if you want it to. I'd like to share how I've used Sass to build responsive, HiDPI-capable projects, and how it once again makes the heavy lifting quite manageable.

NESTED MEDIA QUERIES

One of the foundations of building responsive websites is the CSS media query. The ability to "listen" to the browser's viewport for varying dimensions and then apply certain styles based on those dimensions is the cornerstone of creating flexible layouts that adapt to different devices.

For instance, you may want to adjust the width of a containing element should the browser be less than 800 pixels wide, using a media query:

```
section.main {
  float: left;
  width: 65%;
  font-size: 16px;
  line-height: 1.4;
}
@media screen and (max-width: 800px) {
  section.main {
    float: none;
    width: auto;
  }
}
```

In Sass, you can nest media queries inside the original declaration, and they will "bubble up" into their own separate declarations when the stylesheet is compiled. It's wonderful.

```
section.main {
  float: left;
  width: 65%;
  font-size: 16px;
  line-height: 1.4;

  @media screen and (max-width: 800px) {
    float: none;
    width: auto;
  }

  @media screen and (max-width: 500px) {
    font-size: 12px;
    line-height: 1.4;
  }
}
```

The above will compile to:

```
section.main {
  float: left;
  width: 65%;
  font-size: 16px;
  line-height: 1.4;
}
@media screen and (max-width: 800px) {
  section.main {
    float: none;
    width: auto;
  }
}
@media screen and (max-width: 500px) {
  section.main {
    font-size: 12px;
    line-height: 1.4;
  }
}
```

Nesting media queries avoids rewriting the selector (section.main in this example) each time you'd like to make adjustments for various breakpoints.

It's also immensely convenient that the media-query declarations slot right under the original selector. I've found it much easier to understand what's happening to an element under varying viewports by having the media queries nearby in context, rather than gathered at the end of the stylesheet or in a separate document.

Using variables to define breakpoints

Media-query bubbling is a wonderful convenience that Sass brings to responsive design, but there is still quite a bit of repetition. In each declaration, we're specifying the breakpoints (800px and 500px in the previous example). Often while designing, I tweak those breakpoints based on the particular design I'm working on and observations on how the layout reacts, instead of relying on static device widths. In other words, those breakpoints that you're specifying in each nested media query could change. It'd be great to define those once and be able to edit them in one spot. Sass variables to the rescue!

Let's create some variables for three breakpoints we'll use in our media queries. I'm going to name them something flexible and not tied down to a specific device or finite value.

```
$width-small:   500px;
$width-medium:  800px;
$width-large:   1200px;
```

With the breakpoints defined as Sass variables, we can (as of Sass 3.2) refer to these whenever we use nested media queries throughout the document. For example:

```
section.main {
  font-size: 16px;
  line-height: 1.4;

  @media screen and (max-width: $width-large) {
    float: left;
    width: 65%;
  }

  @media screen and (max-width: $width-medium) {
    float: none;
    width: auto;
  }

  @media screen and (max-width: $width-small) {
    font-size: 12px;
    line-height: 1.4;
  }
}
```

Which will compile to:

```
section.main {
  font-size: 16px;
  line-height: 1.4;

  @media screen and (max-width: 1200px) {
    float: left;
    width: 65%;
  }

  @media screen and (max-width: 800px) {
    float: none;
    width: auto;
  }

  @media screen and (max-width: 500px) {
    font-size: 12px;
    line-height: 1.4;
  }
}
```

If we later decide to tweak those breakpoints, we need only edit the variables once, and Sass will take care of updating them wherever we used them.

```
$width-small:   400px;
$width-medium:  760px;
$width-large:   1100px;
```

This helps tremendously during the initial development of a responsive design, when those breakpoints are a moving target depending on the design requirements and the way the design needs to adapt.

Even math is possible here, as we can add to or subtract from the breakpoint's value:

```
@media screen and (max-width: $width-small + 1) {
  font-size: 12px;
  line-height: 1.4;
}
```

Will compile to:

```
@media screen and (max-width: 401px) {
  font-size: 12px;
  line-height: 1.4;
}
```

While:

```
@media screen and (max-width: $width-small - 1) {
  font-size: 12px;
  line-height: 1.4;
}
```

Will compile to:

```
@media screen and (max-width: 399px) {
  font-size: 12px;
  line-height: 1.4;
}
```

Going a step further, you can also define an entire media query as a variable (not just the numeric value):

```
$mobile-first: "screen and (min-width: 300px)";

@media #{$mobile-first} {
  #content {
    font-size: 14px;
    line-height: 1.5;
  }
}
```

Notice the interpolation brackets—#{}—surrounding the $mobile-first variable. That's a special way to alert Sass to compile something within a selector or property name.

The above SCSS will compile to:

```
@media screen and (min-width: 300px) {
  #content {
    font-size: 14px;
    line-height: 1.5;
  }
}
```

When you nest media queries within the declarations they affect, variables save you a ton of repetition. But we can even simplify things further with @content blocks, also introduced in Sass 3.2.

Combining @content blocks and mixins

By using Sass's @content directive, you can pass entire blocks of styles to a mixin, and Sass will place those blocks back into the declaration that calls the mixin. That sounds confusing, but in practice it's simple and handy.

Let's create a responsive mixin that handles three different breakpoints, with @content placeholders for whatever styles we'd like to include for each breakpoint. We'll also use variables to define the small, medium, and large breakpoint widths as we did earlier in the chapter.

```
$width-small:  400px;
$width-medium: 760px;
$width-large:  1200px;

@mixin responsive($width) {
  @if $width == wide-screens {
    @media only screen and (max-width: $width-large) { »
      @content; }
  }
  @else if $width == medium-screens {
    @media only screen and (max-width: $width-medium) »
      { @content; }
  }
```

```
@else if $width == small-screens {
  @media only screen and (max-width: $width-small) { »
    @content; }
}
}
```

Notice Sass also supports @if and @else statements, which we're using to evaluate the $width variable we'll pass when including the mixin. For example, if we pass the mixin the medium-screens variable, Sass will compile the media query with our max-width set to the $width-medium variable (760px). The @content placeholder allows us to further pass blocks of styles to the mixin that get inserted inside the media query.

With this single mixin set up, we can now call it from any declaration using a compact pattern that reflects the way we think about things:

```
#content {
  float: left;
  width: 70%;
  @include responsive(wide-screens) {
    width: 80%;
  }
  @include responsive(medium-screens) {
    width: 50%;
    font-size: 14px;
  }
  @include responsive(small-screens) {
    float: none;
    width: 100%;
    font-size: 12px;
  }
}
```

Which will compile to:

```
#content {
  float: left;
  width: 70%;
}
@media only screen and (max-width: 1200px) {
  #content {
    width: 80%;
  }
}
@media only screen and (max-width: 760px) {
  #content {
    width: 50%;
    font-size: 14px;
  }
}
@media only screen and (max-width: 400px) {
  #content {
    float: none;
    width: 100%;
    font-size: 12px;
  }
}
```

Magical! Sass feeds any styles to the appropriate media query and reconstructs the declaration with everything in its right place. Using @content blocks for writing contextually-placed media queries makes responsive design a heck of a lot simpler—with less repetition.

It's also easier to grasp how an element will be adjusted across device widths—such as how a heading's font size will vary as the width of the viewport narrows. The entire progression is spelled out in one spot:

```
h1 {
  font-size: 40px;
  @include responsive(wide-screens)   { font-size: »
    48px; }
```

```
@include responsive(medium-screens) { font-size: »
   32px; }
@include responsive(small-screens)  { font-size: »
   20px; }
}
```

Which will compile to:

```
h1 {
  font-size: 40px;
}
@media only screen and (max-width: 1200px) {
  h1 {
    font-size: 48px;
  }
}
@media only screen and (max-width: 760px) {
  h1 {
    font-size: 32px;
  }
}
@media only screen and (max-width: 400px) {
  h1 {
    font-size: 20px;
  }
}
```

Keep the output in mind

It's important to point out that this method results in a lot of
repeated media queries for each selector in the compiled CSS.
Ideally, Sass would let us nest the queries to keep the contextual
connection of rules collected in one space, but then group shared
media query rules when compiled.

For example:

```
blockquote {
  width: 100%;
  @include responsive(wide-screens) { width: 80%; }
}
figure {
  margin: 0 0 20px 0;
  @include responsive(wide-screens) { margin: 0 0 »
    30px 0; }
}
```

Would compile more efficiently, with shared rules wrapped
into one media query:

```
blockquote {
  width: 100%;
}
figure {
  margin: 0 0 20px 0;
}

@media only screen and (max-width: 1200px) {
  blockquote {
    width: 80%;
  }
  figure {
    margin: 0 0 30px 0;
  }
}
```

For a large stylesheet that uses responsive design with frequent media queries for multiple viewports, this would reduce
the compiled CSS file quite a bit. Unfortunately, Sass doesn't
(yet?) support this "aggregated media query bubbling," as I'm
coining it, but for most projects, the trade-off of a slightly larger
compiled stylesheet is worth the ease and sensibility of nesting
media queries inline. So for now, that's how we'll roll.

FIG 4.1–FIG 4.2: Normal-resolution logo on the left, HiDPI version on the right.

"RETINIZING" HIDPI BACKGROUND IMAGES

As if things weren't complicated enough for us web designers, the rise of High Dots Per Inch (HiDPI) screens has created another challenge. Apple's gorgeous Retina screens, for example, squeeze twice the number of pixels compared to that of a normal display. That means beautiful clarity and saying goodbye to fuzzy pixels! But only if you take the time to create graphics that reflect this super-sharp new world.

For `<img>` elements on the page, this typically means creating images twice as large and compressing them to half their size by using the `width` attribute in the markup. Alternatively, there are craftier ways to handle selective image-serving via media queries and JavaScript, such as Scott Jehl's brilliant Picturefill project (http://bkaprt.com/sass/14/).

To share an example of handling HiDPI images, let's take a look at the Sasquatch Records logo, which is 133×121 pixels (**FIG 4.1**). For devices that support the extra pixels, we'll create a second version that's twice as large (266×242) and reduce it to 133 pixels in the markup for twice the clarity (**FIG 4.2**):

```
<img src="-/img/logo-peek-2x.png" width="133" />
```

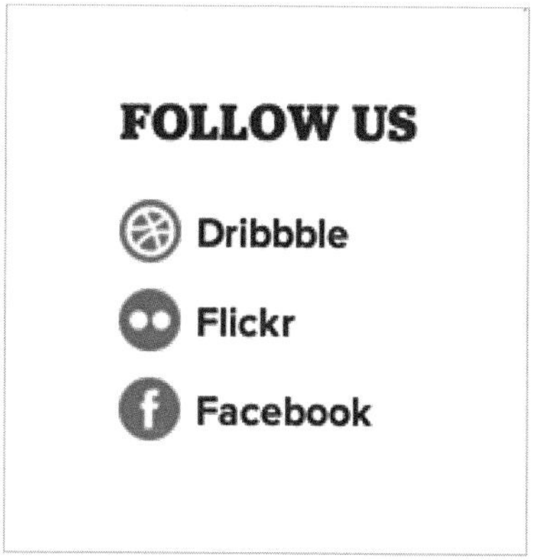

FOLLOW US

 Dribbble

 Flickr

 Facebook

FIG 4.3: Social network links in the sidebar of the Sasquatch Records site.

For background images, we simply use CSS media queries (in modern browsers that support them) to determine whether the display is HiDPI and render the appropriately sized image.

On the Sasquatch Records site, for instance, we have a little list of social network links in the sidebar. Each link's icon has a background image specified in the stylesheet (**FIG 4.3**).

In the Dribbble link, the CSS to align a normal-resolution icon to the left of the text might look like this:

```
ul.follow li.dribbble a {
  padding-left: 30px;
  background-repeat: no-repeat;
  background-position: 0 50%;
  background-image: url(../img/icon-dribbble.png);
}
```

For HiDPI displays, we override the icon with one that is twice as large, and then "squeeze" it down to the right dimensions using the CSS3 background-size property. To detect whether the display is HiDPI, we use a media query and the min-device-pixel-ratio property in CSS3 (which varies depending on the browser vendor).

FIG 4.4: Crisp, Hi-DPI icons by the power of Sass!

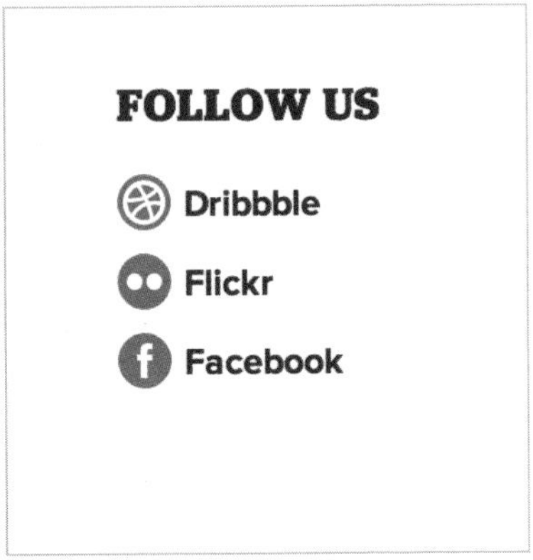

FOLLOW US

 Dribbble

 Flickr

 Facebook

```
@media (-webkit-min-device-pixel-ratio: 1.5),
       (min--moz-device-pixel-ratio: 1.5),
       (-o-min-device-pixel-ratio: 3/2),
       (min-device-pixel-ratio: 1.5),
       (min-resolution: 1.5dppx) {
  ul.follow li.dribbble a {
    padding-left: 30px;
    background-repeat: no-repeat;
    background-position: 0 50%;
    background-image: url(../img/icon-dribbble-2x.png);
    -webkit-background-size: 24px 24px;
       -moz-background-size: 24px 24px;
            background-size: 24px 24px;
  }
}
```

Essentially, we're saying that if the display's pixel ratio is at least 1.5 times the normal density, let's use a larger, 48×48 icon (icon-dribbble-2x.png) and squash it down to 24×24 when displayed on the screen.

The difference, when viewed on a HiDPI display, is stunningly sharp. All those fuzzy edges disappear (**FIG 4.4**).

As you can imagine, "retinizing" your interfaces can result in a pile of repetition, referencing that media query and a second image every time you'd like to override your normal-resolution background images. Here's where Sass can make this process rather painless.

We can create a Sass mixin that handles all the heavy lifting, even forming two different file names with a bit of crafty concatenation.

Here's the retinize mixin I use in my everyday projects—I'll break down each important section.

```
@mixin retinize($file, $type, $width, $height) {
  background-image: url('../img/' + $file + '.' »
    + $type);

  @media (-webkit-min-device-pixel-ratio: 1.5),
         (min--moz-device-pixel-ratio: 1.5),
         (-o-min-device-pixel-ratio: 3/2),
         (min-device-pixel-ratio: 1.5),
         (min-resolution: 1.5dppx) {
    & {
      background-image: url('../img/' + $file + '-2x.' »
        + $type);
      -webkit-background-size: $width $height;
        -moz-background-size: $width $height;
             background-size: $width $height;
    }
  }
}
```

The first line of the mixin sets up the four arguments we need to build the right compiled code:

- The file name
- The type of image (JPG, GIF, PNG)
- Image width on screen
- Image height on screen

Those four arguments are listed like so:

```
@mixin retinize($file, $type, $width, $height) {
```

Calling the retinize mixin is as simple as plugging in those four values anytime you'd like. For example, let's call the mixin for the Dribbble icon, a PNG that should be rendered at 24×24:

```
li.dribbble a {
  @include retinize('icon-dribbble', 'png', 24px, 24px);
}
li.flickr a {
  @include retinize('icon-flickr', 'png', 24px, 24px);
}
li.facebook a {
  @include retinize('icon-facebook', 'png', 24px, 24px);
}
```

Back to the mixin itself, the second line forms the normal-resolution background-image rule by stringing the arguments together. Sass can concatenate!

```
background-image: url('../img/' + $file + '.' + $type);
```

We're adding the file path to the image, then adding the file name and the period and the file type, which will compile like this:

```
background-image: url(../img/icon-dribbble.png);
```

With the normal background image in place, we'll now add the media query that will override that image with the @2× version for devices that support a 1.5 pixel ratio or higher. Again, we're including all the vendor-prefixed properties to ensure this will work across as many browsers as possible.

```
@mixin retinize($file, $type, $width, $height) {
  background-image: url('../img/' + $file + '.' »
    + $type);

  @media (-webkit-min-device-pixel-ratio: 1.5),
         (min--moz-device-pixel-ratio: 1.5),
         (-o-min-device-pixel-ratio: 3/2),
         (min-device-pixel-ratio: 1.5),
         (min-resolution: 1.5dppx) {
    & {
      background-image: url('../img/' + $file + '-2x.' »
        + $type);
    }
  }
}
```

Next we need a way to reference whatever selector we're applying this media query to, and that depends on where we've called the mixin from. Fortunately, we can use the special & placeholder, which you'll remember from the previous chapter, and which inserts whatever the "current selector" is. (In our example case, it's li.dribbble a).

```
@mixin retinize($file, $type, $width, $height) {
  background-image: url('../img/' + $file + '.' »
    + $type);

  @media (-webkit-min-device-pixel-ratio: 1.5),
         (min--moz-device-pixel-ratio: 1.5),
         (-o-min-device-pixel-ratio: 3/2),
         (min-device-pixel-ratio: 1.5),
         (min-resolution: 1.5dppx) {
    & {
      background-image: url('../img/' + $file + '-2x.' »
        + $type);
    }
  }
}
```

Notice also that we're using Sass's concatenation ability to append a `-2x` to the file name to refer to the larger image. It's a good idea to settle on a naming convention like this—a short bit of text that makes managing assets and calling file names in Sass easier:

- Normal image: `file-name.png`
- @2× image for HiDPI: `file-name-2x.png`

You don't need to use `-2x`; you can use whatever you'd like: `file-name-jumbo`, `file-name-twice-as-big`, `file-name-at-two-times`, etc. But I think `-2x` works just fine.

The final piece of the mixin is the `background-size` property (and its `-webkit-` and `-moz-` prefixed equivalents), which tells the browser what dimensions it's going to stuff that larger image into:

```scss
@mixin retinize($file, $type, $width, $height) {
    background-image: url('../img/' + $file + '.' »
    + $type);

    @media (-webkit-min-device-pixel-ratio: 1.5),
           (min--moz-device-pixel-ratio: 1.5),
           (-o-min-device-pixel-ratio: 3/2),
           (min-device-pixel-ratio: 1.5),
           (min-resolution: 1.5dppx) {
        & {
            background-image: url('../img/' + $file + '-2x.' »
            + $type);
            -webkit-background-size: $width $height;
            -moz-background-size: $width $height;
            background-size: $width $height;
        }
    }
}
```

And that's it—a reusable mixin for serving HiDPI background images from any selector you'd like, just by creating two image assets and one line of SCSS:

```
li.dribbble a {
  @include retinize('icon-dribbble', 'png', 24px, 24px);
}
```

Mixins inside mixins!

Mixins can include other mixins. A mixinception, if you will. Don't worry, the universe won't explode! In fact, we can go a step further in DRY-ing up this code, extracting the vendor-prefixed `min-device-pixel-ratio` rules into a variable and the `background-size` property stack into its own mixin. Then these extracted parts could be reused in other sections of the stylesheet or additional mixins. The other advantage here is keeping any vendor-prefixed properties in one spot so we can edit or prune them if the specs change, or once prefixes are no longer necessary (and won't that be a celebratory day).

First, let's replace the pixel-ratio portion of the media query with a reusable variable. As mentioned earlier in the chapter, a variable that appears within a selector needs special interpolation characters around it:

```
@mixin retinize($file, $type, $width, $height) {
  background-image: url('../img/' + $file + '.' »
    + $type);

  @media #{$is-hidpi} {
    & {
      background-image: url('../img/' + $file + '-2x.' »
        + $type);
      -webkit-background-size: $width $height;
        -moz-background-size: $width $height;
            background-size: $width $height;
    }
  }
}
```

Then we'll define that variable with the stack of pixel-ratio rules, which is also reusable elsewhere in the stylesheet if needed:

```
$is-hidpi: "(-webkit-min-device-pixel-ratio: 1.5), »
  (min--moz-device-pixel-ratio: 1.5), »
  (-o-min-device-pixel-ratio: 3/2), »
  (min-device-pixel-ratio: 1.5),(min-resolution: »
  1.5dppx)";
```

Next, let's create a mixin for background-size that takes a width and height attribute and includes the vendor-prefixed properties as well as the "real," un-prefixed one. Anytime we want to use background-size on a selector, we can now call this mixin:

```
@mixin background-size($width, $height) {
  -webkit-background-size: $width $height;
    -moz-background-size: $width $height;
         background-size: $width $height;
}
```

Let's include this background-size mixin within the retinize mixin, passing along the $width and $height variables it's already collecting:

```
@mixin retinize($file, $type, $width, $height) {
  background-image: url('../img/' + $file + '.' »
    + $type);

  @media #{$is-hidpi} {
    & {
      background-image: url('../img/' + $file + '-2x.' »
        + $type);
      @include background-size($width, $height);
    }
  }
}
```

And there you have it. We've refactored the original retinize mixin to include code that can be reused in additional styles or mixins. That'll reduce the amount of repetition throughout our Sass code, and keep shared styles in as few places as possible for future updates and maintenance.

WRAPPING UP

I hope this little pink book has helped you get started with Sass and become familiar with its core features. I also hope that it's dispelled some of the misunderstandings that Sass sometimes bears:

- You have to learn Ruby.
- You need to change your entire CSS process.
- You need to be an expert with the command line.

As we've discussed, it's much simpler than that. But Sass can be as powerful as you want it to be. At the least, it's a fantastic tool that can fit nicely beside your systems and workflow without disturbing the CSS you've been writing for years (or if you've only been writing CSS for months, well then…months—and bravo!).

Now go simplify your stylesheets with reusable blocks of Sassy CSS, save yourself a boatload of time, and, most important, build awesome things!

RESOURCES

Websites and articles

- **Sass reference:** The official documentation for all things Sass
- (http://bkaprt.com/sass/15/).
- **The Sass Way:** "...covers the latest news and topics on crafting CSS using Sass and Compass." Great articles and resources on how to best put Sass to use (http://bkaprt.com/sass/16/).
- **CSS Tricks:** Chris Coyier has covered Sass pretty extensively, and we share very similar views on how Sass can help the CSS hand-coder (http://bkaprt.com/sass/17/). In particular, be sure to check out his Sass Style Guide (http://bkaprt.com/sass/18/).
- **Assembling Sass:** Code School's comprehensive course on learning Sass, soup to nuts (http://bkaprt.com/sass/19/).
- **Getting started with Sass:** Great intro article on *A List Apart* by David Demaree (http://bkaprt.com/sass/20/).
- **Looking into the future of Sass:** David Walsh assesses what's coming down the pipeline for future Sass features. Lots of great insight on where Sass is headed (http://bkaprt.com/sass/21/).

Mixin libraries

- **Compass:** An extensive framework for Sass created by Chris Eppstein. Even if you're not using Compass, the documentation is a goldmine for mixin ideas (http://bkaprt.com/sass/22/).
- **Bourbon:** Billing itself as "A simple and lightweight mixin library for Sass," Bourbon offers a ton of great mixin concepts from fellow Bostonians, thoughtbot (http://bkaprt.com/sass/23/).
- **Handy Sass Mixins:** A nice collection of Sass mixins from Jake Bresnehan (http://bkaprt.com/sass/24/).

More Sass and responsive design

In particular, these two articles on responsive web design in Sass and media queries helped me craft Chapter 4 (http://bkaprt.com/sass/25/, http://bkaprt.com/sass/26/).

- **Breakpoint:** A plugin for Sass that makes writing media queries even simpler (http://bkaprt.com/sass/27/).
- **Susy:** A helper for Compass and Sass for creating responsive grid systems (http://bkaprt.com/sass/28/).
- **Sassaparilla:** A kick-start framework for creating responsive web design projects using Compass and Sass. Also has a great name (http://bkaprt.com/sass/29/).

Sass tools

- **FireSass for Firebug:** A handy Firefox add-on that will display the original Sass filename and line number of Sass-compiled stylesheets, for debugging (http://bkaprt.com/sass/30/).
- **Developing with Sass and Chrome DevTools:** A tutorial on how to best use Chrome while developing with Sass. Some of it is experimental, but you can bet more of this kind of thing will emerge as Sass continues to gain steam (http://bkaprt.com/sass/31/).

Other CSS preprocessors

While Sass is the subject of this little book, it's not the only CSS preprocessor out there. If you've caught the preprocessing bug (and I surely hope you have), it might be worth checking out these alternatives—noting how they differ from Sass.

LESS

LESS is another popular choice for designers and front-end craftspeople. It's very similar to Sass in that it also supports variables, mixins, and other functions, but it uses a slightly different syntax. Like Sass's SCSS, LESS is an extension of CSS, which means it plays nicely with existing stylesheets and can be gradually folded in (http://bkaprt.com/sass/32/).

LESS also has a client-side option for compiling, which serves .less files to the browser that JavaScript compiles into regular CSS when the page loads. It's a handy way to work locally and in development, as no command line or app needs to run the conversion for you. However, client-side compiling is not recommended for production sites.

Like Sass, LESS has a command-line program as well as third-party apps that convert LESS files into CSS files.

Feature-wise, in comparison to Sass, LESS does a little...well, less. From my perspective, Sass has a more active development cycle and community behind it, and is a bit more robust in its functionality. That said, what LESS does support is the important stuff—features that will help you write DRY stylesheets more efficiently. You're already winning if you're using a preprocessor, regardless of which one.

For a great comparison of Sass versus LESS, have a gander at Chris Coyier's thorough article, in which he breaks down the differences and pros and cons (http://bkaprt.com/sass/33/).

These debates can at times become religious warfare, but the key thing is to use what you're most comfortable with. Both will help immensely in easing the creation of smart stylesheets.

Stylus

Stylus is a bit younger than LESS and Sass, and it has a broad feature set. Its syntax is more like Sass's original syntax (optional indenting, optional omission of braces and semicolons). I like tools that don't alter my normal workflow too much, so for that reason I haven't checked out Stylus extensively. But I'm mentioning it here because, again, if it feels right for you, then go for it. The important thing is to take advantage of one of these tools to make your life a little easier (http://bkaprt.com/sass/34/).

REFERENCES

Shortened URLs are numbered sequentially; the related long URLs are listed below for reference.

Chapter 1

1 http://pragprog.com/the-pragmatic-programmer
2 http://c2.com/cgi/wiki?DontRepeatYourself
3 http://www.w3.org/People/Bos/DesignGuide/maintainability.html
4 http://sass-lang.com/about.html

Chapter 2

5 http://rubyinstaller.org
6 http://mhs.github.com/scout-app/
7 http://incident57.com/codekit
8 http://livereload.com
9 http://compass.handlino.com

Chapter 3

10 http://blog.engineyard.com/2011/front-end-maintainability-with-sass-and-style-guides
11 http://www.w3.org/TR/css-variables/
12 http://compass-style.org
13 http://bourbon.io/

Chapter 4

14 https://github.com/scottjehl/picturefill

Resources

15 http://sass-lang.com/docs/yardoc/file.SASS_REFERENCE.html
16 http://thesassway.com
17 http://css-tricks.com/search-results/?q=sass
18 http://css-tricks.com/sass-style-guide/
19 http://www.codeschool.com/courses/assembling-sass

20 http://alistapart.com/article/getting-started-with-sass

21 http://davidwalsh.name/future-sass

22 http://compass-style.org/reference/compass/

23 http://bourbon.io

24 http://web-design-weekly.com/2013/05/12/handy-sass-mixins/

25 http://thesassway.com/intermediate/responsive-web-design-in-sass-using-media-queries-in-sass-32

26 http://css-tricks.com/media-queries-sass-3-2-and-codekit/

27 https://github.com/Team-Sass/breakpoint

28 http://susy.oddbird.net

29 http://sass.fffunction.co

30 https://addons.mozilla.org/en-us/firefox/addon/firesass-for-firebug/

31 http://net.tutsplus.com/tutorials/html-css-techniques/developing-with-sass-and-chrome-devtools/

32 http://lesscss.org

33 http://css-tricks.com/sass-vs-less/

34 http://learnboost.github.io/stylus/

ACKNOWLEDGEMENTS

First and most importantly, I need to thank my partner in crime at Dribbble, Rich Thornett. Rich cured my reluctance in using Sass by way of relentless prodding and evangelism while we worked on our little design community. It only took a whole year. Thanks for being persistent, Rich!

I'd also like to thank A Book Apart for allowing me another go around here. They are a fantastic team, and quite frankly make it difficult to think of writing anywhere else. To Mandy Brown, Jason Santa Maria, and Jeffrey Zeldman—thanks for creating something wonderful for both readers *and* authors.

Special thanks to Managing Director Katel LeDu. You've kept everything shipshape, and that ain't always easy. Such a pleasure working with you.

To Erin Kissane, thank you for making me sound like a better writer than I actually am. It's been an honor to have you do that. And to Jina Bolton for being a wonderful technical editor and ambassador for Sass.

A gigantic thanks to Hampton Catlin for inventing Sass, and Nathan Weizenbaum and Chris Eppstein for developing Sass and making it the indispensable tool that it is today.

And finally, thanks to you, for reading.

INDEX

R

retina screens 80
retinize mixin 83

S

Sass
    definition of 14
    syntax 15
SCSS ("Sassy CSS") 15
style guides, creating 41

T

Thomas, Dave 12
thoughtbot 61

V

variables 40
    defining 40
    in CSS 43
viewports, multiple 75

W

watch command 22

ABOUT A BOOK APART

We cover the emerging and essential topics in web design and development with style, clarity, and above all, brevity—because working designer-developers can't afford to waste time.

COLOPHON

The text is set in FF Yoga and its companion, FF Yoga Sans, both by Xavier Dupré. Headlines and cover are set in Titling Gothic by David Berlow.

MIX
Paper from responsible sources
FSC® C103203
FSC www.fsc.org

This book was printed in the United States using FSC certified Finch papers.